WE ALL SHARE THE
CHALLENGE
TO ENTER THE
ABYSS
TAME OUR
DEMONS
DISCOVER OUR
POWER
AND RETURN WITH
THE LIGHT

BEEN

Hidden Treasures of the Appalachian Highlands

BRIAN S. WOODS

"CALL ME THE TAKER
OF THE ARDUOUS TREK...

... A SEEKER OF THE
ULTIMATE TRACK"

B E E N

HIDDEN TREASURES OF THE APPALACHIAN HIGHLANDS

BY

BRIAN S WOODS

ISBN: 9798787457650

Imprint: Independently published

Produced, ARRANGED, composed,

& PHOTOGRAPHY by BRIAN S WOODS

Dedicated to the Dobson's (Rick and LaDonna), who convinced me to put it into action

And to my mother, who convinced me to put it into words

TABLE OF CONTENTS

A Long Time Ago in a Land Far, Far Away ...

Powell Valley, Virginia

Appearances are but the decoy; it is where one disappears that reveals one's true nature ~

A speleologist is a scientist of karsts (caves formed in limestone). This is the professional whom you might find studying bat species, the direction water flowed during paleo times when a slit began opening, or the type of limestone of which a cave is composed. Speleologists are experts in geology, hydrology, biology, and caves.

A caver is an amateur who explores karsts. Ranging from beginner to expert, a caver engages crawling and squeezing through tights places, climbing, or rappelling into vertical pits, mapping the depths or scuba diving in a lake of absolute darkness, miles within a mountain.

So, while nearly all speleologists are cavers, only a small percentage of cavers are speleologists.

I know quite a bit about science, but do not profess nor have the qualifications to be a speleologist. In caves, I have crawled, squeezed, climbed, descended, and swam in places few are willing to brave … but there are much truer cavers than I. What I am is a scarcer breed: a searcher … a finder. Before a speleologist can study, before a caver can map a new passage, someone must first find the cave. That someone is me. For decades, I have searched for undocumented caves (by *undocumented*, meaning previously undiscovered, long forgotten, or known by a limited few, such as a landowner). Almost always, this involves reaching and probing areas that range in difficulty from inhospitable to nearly inaccessible. Success doesn't happen often, but when it does … (expletive)!

In the mid-1970's, by the age of nine, I was exploring the rolling fields, low woodlands, and mountainous forests near and along the easter rim of Powell Valley, located in Wise County, itself nestled in the southwest corner of Virginia. Almost always, these explorations occurred alone. My family lived several miles from the nearest town, itself with a small population. Homes were separated by pastures, woods, and often marked by barbed wire fences. There were few kids my age, fewer were friends, and even fewer with similar drive and interest. As I grew, so did the distances of exploration, its duration, and difficulty. Day and often by night, regardless of season or weather conditions, I freely roamed.

My generation was the last to grow up without computers, cell phones, or even cable tv. The internet did not exist, as neither did social media nor GPS (Global Positioning System). Whatever interests one might have, there were few resources from which to learn and no social connections to share. Experiences occurred independent of the world. My adventurous lessons were self-taught, close calls were unspoken, and wonders only rarely photographed or otherwise shared. Events like swimming through snake-infested ponds at night, being chased up a tree by wild dogs, or simply roaming places off the grid (i.e., no one on earth knows where you are) were routine experiences that lacked any desire to be shared.

I was taught hunting, trapping, fishing, and gigging. Of these, I was competent but enjoyed none. Indeed, it was the study of natural sciences, Native Americans, finding fossils, exploring forest, and searching for caves that became my life's interests and passions. My parents, recognizing these traits, afforded me with experiences, books, and studies. Such included a monthlong tour of national parks, several summers at Nature Camp, Inc. (a two-week study of natural sciences, located in the George Washington National Forest near Vesuvius, Virginia), and a college Caving course, taught by renowned caver, Roy D. Powers, Jr. Even friends and neighbors were supportive. For example, Dr. Lawrence J. Fleenor, Jr. (author of *The Bear Grass*, an informative history of southwest Virginia) and his wife, Betty Fleenor, allowed me to walk across their ranch for quicker access to Powell Mountain

It was a compelling upbringing that might have ended upon reaching adulthood. The downside of growing up in rural America is that jobs can be few, and many of its youth are drawn to larger towns and cities for greater career opportunities. Indeed, today, the populations of most southwest Virginia counties are stagnant (some even in decline). I was an example of that dynamic by moving away to college and pursuing other places. Travels, experiences, pleasures, adventures, and explorations expanded elsewhere. Life evolved and maturity eventually settled in. I married, bought a home, became a parent, and began a career (By the way, responsibility is just another form of challenge and adventure!).

For another twenty years, my parents continued to live at our Virginia home. My visits were periodic but nearly always included brief excursions into the same childhood roams. When my parents finally moved away (to a similarly remote and mountainous setting in Tennessee), it begged the question, 'Had the connection finally been cut?' Nope, it had not.

Indeed, despite the evolution of my life, childhood passions remained, and a recurrent dream never ceased: Powell Mountain, specifically the section adjacent to our home, was hollow, people lived inside, and openings lined the cliffs. For those familiar with the movie *Close Encounters of the Third Kind,* Powell Mountain had always been my Devil's Tower.

Instead of never returning, my explorations to Powell Valley not only continued, but expanded. Now living only an hour away, adventure could be had any given weekend. With the aid of the internet, I could access past studies, understand the area with better knowledge and perspective. With Google Earth, I could study from above., pursue areas of interest, and systematically search. The lure of finding that forgotten or that never found still flowed within my veins. And so, those adventures of a long time ago, in a land far, far away, began anew.

Unbeknownst to me, during this same time, cavers had broken through a blocked passage of a known Powell Mountain cave (just outside the reach at that point of my own explorations), revealing a much longer passage. This prompted further investigations, and with these, more passageways were revealed until it became apparent that a major cave system had been discovered. Now known as the *Omega Cave System*, it is the largest in Virginia, and, as exploration continues, Omega's size keeps on growing.

The depths of Omega extend across the very section of Powell Mountain adjacent to our home. My dreams had been correct in at least one aspect: the mountain, indeed, was hollow.

So, you now understand why it is fitting that **BEEN: HIDDEN TREASURES OF THE APPALACHIAN HIGHLANDS**, devotes a chapter to the eastern rim of Powell Valley. This is where the story began, developed, endured, and likely shall continue.

Yet, let's first describe the greater region Powell Valley occupies, a place known as the *Appalachian Highlands* …

APPALACHIAN HIGHLANDS

Grant me deeps and peaks, for I struggle with pleasantries, am subdued in ease, and stumbled by mediocrity. It is in the company of deeps and peaks that I am free ~

BEEN contains itself within the region known as the *Appalachian Highlands*, a culturally distinct region that includes the foothills and mountains of southwest-Virginia, western-North Carolina and east-Tennessee. This is my stronghold, and for the last six decades I have traversed the areas that beckoned to be challenged, explored, and experienced.

This book is more of an informal journal of individual experiences than it is a professional guide or textbook. Many articles, books, and studies exist describing various aspects of the complex geology, biodiversity, and unique qualities of the Blue Ridge, Appalachian, and Smoky Mountains (aka Smokey or Smokies). Almost any topic I present has its own available resources. **BEEN** serves not to repeat, but provide a unique personal account, understanding, and photography. Whereas a guide or textbook utilizes material from other sources, this book lacks reference, uses no resources, and borrows no quotes. It relies on my experiences and knowledge (or lack of). It goes it alone, just as I have done for so many years.

The area endures several sensational myths, most are untrue, at least as far as I can tell. Bigfoot does not live here, as neither do secret Melungeon villages, nor active warfare between the Hatfields and McCoys. There is a history of moonshining, coal mining, and poverty. Ultimately, as with any distinct region, it is composed of a unique and good people.

Now, a brief overview of the sections of three States that make up the Appalachian Highlands …

Of the several counties in southwest Virginia, it is Wise County (including the City of Norton) that I am most familiar. For generations, coal mining was its biggest industry. It has long been a rural region, one of steep hills, dark hollows, valleys, and mountain ridges. These are the *Appalachian Mountains*, old and once as high as the Himalayans, yet long-since eroded. Now, a mountain here is a mountain only because it has eroded slower than the surrounding valleys, creating striking and steep 1000 – 2000ft elevation contrasts. The coal mining industry began to decline in the 1980's, and the region has experience population decline since. The natural beauty of the region, long overlooked, has gradually become recognized as the area's most promising means in reviving a dying culture and economy. The land has much potential.

Most often, my treks here involve penetrating dense vegetation, steep inclines, and unstable ground. When available, to offset the expense of energy and time fighting these conditions, I use game trails and manways. *Game Trails* are feint animal pathways (most often deer). The repeated use tends to level and stabilize the ground. *Manways* is term used to describe unofficial pathways, or primitive trails that connected main trails. Back in the day, trails were a primary means in getting from one settlement to the next. Manways, most often used by trail maintenance workers, were a quicker means in accessing another trail. There is a history of logging in these parts, and the remnants of logging roads persist. Feint, often overgrown with trees, these still offer the relief of stabilized ground.

This region has long been largely ignored. The upstate Shenandoah Valley has always drawn more prestige and attention (although the Cumberland Gap, located at the western edge of Virginia, does possess widespread recognition). That is changing. *The Creeper Trail*, located near Damascus and Abingdon, Virginia, has become well known (The *Appalachian Trail* passes through this area). The City of Norton is undergoing earnest efforts in developing trails and outdoor recreation, especially at an area known as High Knob. *High Knob* is a term that refers both to High Knob, at 4223 feet, the highest local elevation, the High Knob Recreation Area, and to a geographic mountainous area of the Jefferson National Forest referred to generally as 'High Knob'. Image change is part of any success in achieving renaissance, High Knob is emblematic.

A prime example of the High Knob makeover is Chief Benge, a half breed Cherokee warrior who terrorized the area until his death in the late-1700's (killed in a skirmish near my childhood home). Back in the day, like many people, I associated Benge with drinking beer (I also associated binging with beer, but that is another story!). Halfway up High Knob from the city of Norton there is a place known as *Benge's Rock*. It was go-at-your-own-risk because it was the rough man's outdoor drinking spot. It was a common sight to see some mean looking characters standing roadside at Benge's Rock. Most likely included would be members of the local biker gang, the *Warlords* (this an actual gang, not a group of weekend warriors). Largely ignored by law enforcement, everyone knew what they were doing.

Today, Chief Benge's image has been cleaned up. Benge's Rock remains, but the beer cans, graffiti, and trash are gone, and the perpetual drinking party disbanded. Better, there is the development of the terrific *Chief Benge Scout Trail,* itself part of a growing network and effort to establish new trails and reestablish historic ones. Indeed, today one can roam the High Knob mountainside much like those in centuries past.

I'm not sure where those mean looking characters went!

The highest mountains east of the Mississippi are in western-North Carolina. Albeit, not has tall as those out West, but impressive by virtue of seemingly endless layers of distant peaks. Indeed, the region here is a maze of steep rises and deep cut gaps.

These are the *Blue Ridge Mountains,* and contrast with southwest-Virginia Appalachians' in three important respects (for me, anyway). First, whereas the Appalachians are composed of sedimentary stone, the Blue Ridge is primarily composed of metamorphic rock. This is harder stone. Walking on it is much firmer. Footholds and handholds are more secure. Secondly, unlike the abundance of caves in southwest Virginia and east Tennessee, few caves exist in this region. Thirdly, alpine evergreen forests, including trees such as hemlock, spruce, fir, and hemlock grow in abundance.

The region abounds with popular, impressive trails, as well as sports and activities associated with the outdoors (skiing, mountain biking, and climbing, for examples). From the Blue Ridge Parkway alone, there is so much to see and experience that books are devoted to it. Mount Mitchell, at 6684ft, is the highest peak east of the Mississippi. Asheville is a major destination, as is Grandfather Mountain. Let's not forget the Appalachian Trail, as its North Carolina section arrives from Tennessee and continues into Virginia.

These mountains are substantial enough to possess independent weather systems. Incredible rains occasionally collide against the peaks, causing flooding and havoc to the valleys below. Streams become raging torrents and can literally wash homes away. High winds occur. Wind speeds on Grandfather Mountain can reach 100 miles per hour.

So rural and rugged, fugitive Eric Rudolph lived in this region for several years, most likely in some combination of living off the land and receiving local assistance. Occasionally, I assisted in the hunt for the FBI's Most Wanted and searched for Rudolph's whereabouts. When he was finally caught, he was healthy, well-clothed, but seemingly relieved to surrender.

Geologically there are three parts that compose east-Tennessee. Towards the north, there are the Appalachian Mountains, composed primarily of shale, slate, and limestone. To the south, the Blue Ridge Mountains, chiefly composed of metamorphic rock (such as quartzite). In between are the rolling hills, rivers and lakes of Tennessee Valley. Combined, the area boasts a variety of elevation, rugged mountains, hills, caves, wildlife, and wetlands.

The Smoky Mountains are the dominate attraction. These are impressive but, personally, I would enjoy the

Smokies (notice the difference in spelling; there is no consensus what the proper spelling is) much more if it was less crowded. Indeed, *The Great Smoky Mountains National Park* has been the most visited park in the United States, attracting millions per year. Sure, there are terrific trails, such as *Mount LeConte* (via *Alum Cave Trail*), *Charlie's Bunion*, and *Mount Cammerer*, but traffic slows access and crowds overwhelm most trails in the area.

From the summit of Mount LeConte

East-Tennessee is correctly associated with black bear, deer, and turkey, as all are in abundance, as are coyote, squirrel, and rabbits. Here, but lesser seen are animals such as the bobcat, beaver, and hawks. Fish include bass, musky, catfish, and trout. So far, wild boar (aka: feral hogs) have not meaningfully accessed the highlands.

Depending on the adventure you seek, it's highly likely there is something for you in the Appalachian Highlands. Since this book, however, is my informal journal, let us veer back to that which, for now, means veering off the trail to discuss off-trail trekking …

Off-Trail Trekking

Bobcat tracks in snow

There is a misconception of those who explore:

it is not answers they seek,

but the longing for another question ~

Ruggedness speaks a language

Seldom heard

Severity tells of a providence

Few understand

In places where mindless chatter has ceased

Silence reigns

And, in the clarity of the struggle

One is cleansed

In the humbleness of perspective

One's vision expands

And found becomes the answer

When questions are left behind ...

I am _not_ a hiker, nor person who likes to camp. My instincts are that of trekking and mountaineering. *Hiking* is its own discipline, mindset - one that involves long hours of waking, usually on pleasant trails, and often with heavy packs/supplies. Camping is self-explanatory. If you are depending on me to tell a good campfire story, then you are in trouble. Instead of sitting by a fire, I much prefer moving through the night. Hikers and campers tend to go in groups. I tend to go alone. *Trekking* implies greater intensity (than hiking) and *Mountaineering* even more, to the point of being athletically-demanding. Together, trekking and mountaineering often feature other skills such as scrambling. For those unfamiliar with the term, *scrambling* is like climbing but, instead of pulling or anchoring into stone (as a climber would), a scrambler uses anything solid enough to push off, balance, or create enough split second 'grip' to reach the next point. A scrambler often uses *all fours* (hand and feet), but might find themselves briefly *free-soloing*, which is climbing without rope, harness, or means of safety. Often, the hardest routes are intentionally chosen. Minimal gear and supplies are taken. Bad weather is a preferred challenge. Treks and mountaineering can be creative. I have combined kayaking, snorkeling, off-trail, ascending a peak, and caving *on the same outing.*

Apart from the Linville Gorge, I'm not sure I ever took to a trail before the age of thirty. It wasn't a matter of frowning upon trails; I was simply oblivious to them. Off-trail was my norm, and it took an embarrassing experience when taking a group of experienced hikers off-trail that I understood other norms existed. They were expecting scenic views, epic places … not combat with spider webs, dense foliage, and unsure footing. Intimate with both nowadays, both deserve understanding of commonality …

and of differences. Indeed, the difference between trail and off-trail is extensive, especially in the Appalachians. Off-trail is much more hazardous. Here are several examples:

- **No trail**. The most obvious difference is that there is literally *no trail*. Moving forward require constant decision-making, as one moves over rocks, fallen trees, briars, or dense undergrowth. Often, one must choose going around an area (aka easier to go around) before resuming desired direction (i.e., zig zag, fluid, and dynamic method of moving).
- **Getting lost**. The risk of losing one's sense of direction is greater. Beneath a forest canopy on a cloudy day, with visibility already limited by mountainous terrain, one can get turned around. The ability to navigate is crucial. Knowing the cardinal directions and understanding topographical maps are favorable skills.
- **Trespassing.** Crossing over onto someone's land occurs, even by accident. Homeowners (especially homeowners who use their land to hunt) can be wary and protective of their land. It is possible to unknowingly walk beneath a hunter sitting high on a tree stand. Decades back, stumbling across a moonshine still was a possibility. Later decades, a marijuana patch. These could be risky for a trespasser, as wrongdoers wanted their secrets kept secret. Fortunately, meth production is now in vogue, and producers have no need shake and bake meth in the rugged hideaways.
- **Exposure**. Fatigue, hypothermia, dehydration, heat exhaustion are concerns. Summer temperatures commonly reach into the 90's. Winter temperatures reach single digits. Wind chills often fall below

zero. Then there's humidity, which is high in these parts. Heavy air moisture makes heat hotter, and cold colder.

- **Injuries**. Without a firm, established trail, slips trips and falls are much more likely to occur. On Powell Mountain, hardly anything is firm. Rocks are unstable, footing is slippery, and handholds often are pulled loose. In the summer, dense undergrowth often obscures the ground. As critical as footwork is, feet must learn to 'see' what eyes cannot.
- **Wildlife**. For all the concern over bear and snakes, most issues involve dogs, mosquitos, ticks, bees, and beer drinking 'sportsmen'.
- **Damage.** Especially with ground cover and thick vegetation, it is difficult not to cause damage while walking. Following a path protects the terrain from further harm. Going off-trail can be like becoming a human machete.
- **Off the radar**. No one can find you. With a trail, a search team has a good starting place to find you. Not so with off-trail. By its nature, off-trail is exploratory. You set out north, but if something to the east looks interesting, you might decide to bear east. Mountain climbers peer upwards, study, and choose a deliberate route. They understand what the opportunities the rock is giving them. Off-trail trekking does much the same, yet it is more immediate, fast-paced, kinetic. In this case, it is what opportunity the terrain is giving. Vegetation, rocks, change of pitch, standing water … require deliberation yet improvisation. Study, yet quick thinking. Do I choose crawling beneath the fallen tree, wading through briars, or veering wide to the

right? Cell phone coverage is spotty and cannot be relied upon.

- **Briars and Thickets.** One might think areas where trees have been cut down will offer relief. This is incorrect, as thorns quickly overtake area cleared of shade and trees. Old growth areas by far are the easiest to travel through. That is, unless Mountain Laurel is present. Classified as a tree, *kalmia latifolia* (the wild version of Rhododendron) creates its own thickets of impenetrable maze.

The is an image of one of my most unusual outcrop finds … however, it is on remote private land used for hunting. After trespassing several times, and twice evading a search team mounted on ATVs, I reached out to the owner to seek scheduled permission to explore this area … but was denied. I have since complied and have not returned.

- **Solo Caving:** is its own special category. Solo caving is extreme. There is no room for error, no allowance for a mistake that prevents one from returning to the cave's entrance. There is a saying 'only cavers rescue cavers.' As a solo caver, I have no expectation of rescue. Let me describe entering a cave alone: just a few feet in, your cell phone loses connection to the outer world. The domain is silent and in complete darkness. If something goes wrong, there is no one to help you or go for help. If something goes wrong, and no one knows where you are, no one knows where to search (when you don't show back up). Claustrophobia is not an option. Afraid of heights is not an option. Afraid of darkness not an option. Afraid of bugs or getting muddy? Not an option. Even with a group, a helmet is a necessity. You will bump your head on stone. Several sources of light are a necessity. If your batteries die, then what? Food and water are necessities. A first aid kit geared towards fall-related injuries (falls are most common injury in caves) is a necessity. Recommended: a compass (easy to get turned around, as tunnels tend to look the same). Wool clothing (warm and quick to dry) is advisable.

The attraction of off-trail is that it is exploratory. Creative routes are unlimited. Just be careful not to misjudge distances or time it takes to reach a destination. Have contingencies (i.e., what happens if it rains or becomes dark before you get back to your vehicle?). Precautions allow for greater freedom to enjoy. Success and skill mingle. You may be so good that you are wanting to take it up another level. One of the more fun projects was creative process of transforming the conceptual into action, creating long routes from scratch. One worth mentioning took the form of a very challenging day. Mostly off-trail, it began at *Lonesome Pine Country Club* and ended at the trailhead of the *Devil's Bathtub*.

LPCC TO DEVIL'S BATHTUB

Maiden Voyage: Brian S Woods, Skylr Woods, and Lucas McGinnis

Distance: 13 – 18 miles (depending on departure location, specific route, and pick up rendezvous)

Elevation Gain: >3000 Feet

The concept was this: from the 13th Tee of the Lonesome Pine Country Club, in Powell Valley, Virginia, one enters the forest, heading south. The first major obstacle is an 1800ft ascent of rugged *Sheep Gap*. From there required traveling through National Forest and at least three sections of private property until reaching *Big Cherry Reservoir*. By continuing south, we were able to connect with the outer loop of the *Devil's Fork Loop Trail*. Still several miles from the finish, we traveled counterclockwise, eventually passing Devil's Bathtub, en route to the trailhead (in Fort Blackmore, VA). I've completed this challenge day trek several times.

Easier route in yellow. More difficult route in red. *Image by Google Earth

Devil's Bathtub, a naturally formed deep pool, once a local secret, has become a popular hike. Its trail is primitive, with at least a dozen creek crossings (double, if you return same way), and rated as difficult, much because of the slippery footing. Every year, a few manage to get injured or become lost (there is consideration to reroute the trail to make it easier and less prone for injury). Compared to what we went through in getting there from the country club, the Devil was heavenly easy.

Upstream from Devil's Bathtub (FYI: nearly every image in this book is a cell phone pic)

RECOMMENDED TRAILS, WATER, CAVES + THINGS

As previously mentioned, for the longest time, I didn't know trails (other than Linville Gorge). It was an exciting day when I took a group of experienced hikers off-trail, but it was not what they expected. It was too hazardous, hard, and ended with several of them visibly upset. It prompted me to learn what trails were all about and, for twenty years now, I've grown very intimate with the trails of the Appalachian Highlands. I can cater to every level and desired experience. When it comes to trails and known places of the Appalachian Highlands, these are some of my personal favorites and recommendations. With no certain criteria or rank, here goes:

GRANDFATHER MOUNTAIN

Location: North Carolina (Near Banner Elk, Blowing Rock, Boone, and Linville)

From easy to difficult, there is something for everyone at Grandfather Mountain. *Grandfather Mountain* refers both to a Grandfather Mountain State Park and to the privately-owned Grandfather Mountain Stewardship

Foundation operation adjacent to the State Park. Generally, the State Park is maintained in its primitive, natural state. Trailheads begin in the foothills and ascend to the summit ridge. Of these, *Profile Trail* is a good example. For miles, it slowly winds its way up the mountain before connecting to the upper ridgeline trails. The pro and con of this is that it can sap the energy out of your legs, especially if you are not in tip top shape. The Stewardship Foundation is developed (museum, bathrooms, picnic tables, paved walkways, etc.) and caters much more to the casual tourist than to the serious trekker (not a statement of disrespect; plenty of family and children's activities). There is a reason, however, for those seeking a challenge to pay the entrance fee and park next to those there for a less strenuous day. This reason is known as *Grandfather Trail.*

Grandfather Trail runs the length of the summit ridge and across two notable peaks: *MacRae Peak* and *Calloway Peak.* By beginning here, one is fresh, and can fully engage what is a very athletic trail. By *athletic,* meaning that the trail is a total body exercise that includes quite a bit of hand-over-hand progression with ladders, cables, and rocky cliffs. I was skeptical of the ladders and cables, believing the trail might be a cheesy disappointment. Wrong! The designer(s) must be commended, having managed to perfectly blend difficult with doable, and challenging with exciting. Much of the trail is along the mountain's edge, crossing MacRae and Calloway Peak, and offering breathtaking after breathtaking views.

Bottom line: if you want distance, start from one of the State Park's trailheads. If you want action, pay the entrance fee, and start from the parking area of Grandfather Mountain Stewardship Foundation.

One of several ladders. My skepticism proved unfounded; the ladders did not detract but improved the trail.

Engineered section of Profile Trial

It is a safe trail should you keep focused and work within your abilities. For the careless, over-aggressive, or those who edge out too far (for that perfect Instagram pic), there are plenty places to trip, roll an ankle, or fall.

Weather is often a factor. Be prepared for anything, despite the weather forecast. Summertime storms commonly include lightning strikes (not good, when you're walking along the top of a mountain). Wintertime temperatures and windchill often fall below zero. Then there is the wind. Even on a sunny day, wind is a constant. During storms, be prepared for the spectacular. It is not unheard of for wind speed to exceed 100 miles per hour on Grandfather Mountain.

Here, planes remain at crash site

Linville Gorge

Location: Pisgah National Forest (near Linville, North Carolina)

Linville Gorge is very steep, very deep (over 2000 feet deep in several areas), and with an abundance of rock outcrops, huge boulders, and high cliffs. At the bottom runs the Linville River. Other than the tourist-friendly Linville Falls Trail, the trails on the gorge are primitive. Enthusiasm can get the best of some, and it is not unusual to learn of those getting lost, injured, or killed. I recall hearing of one person whose body was not found for several months. That is not surprising, for the terrain is nothing if not rugged and unforgiving.

Basically, there are the west rim trails and the east rim trails. Most of the west rim trails are descents into the bottom of the gorge. These are short, steep trails that connect to the Linville River Trail, which runs parallel to the river. Often, I go down one trail, connect to the river trail, and ascend a different trail.

East rim trails differ. There is more variety in the location of trailheads. Some begin as ascents, some descend. *Table Rock Trail* (outstanding vistas) begins near its summit. Some, such as *The Chimneys* skirt along the top of the ridges (outstanding view of rugged terrain).

When I began trekking the gorge back in the 1990's, it was mostly an evergreen forest, dominated by gigantic hemlock trees. That changed with the infestation of the Wooly Adelgid, an invasive Asian insect that is attracted to hemlocks and feeds off its sap. Without its natural predators, the insect has spread unrestrained. The result has been a massive hemlock die-off, and only a small percentage of these magnificent trees remain.

Often associated with Linville Gorge is the phenomena called *The Brown Mountain Lights*. Often described as "orbs," these lights are unexplained phenomena that appear low in the air under favorable atmospheric (after a rain, I am told) conditions, slowly rise above ground, and then linger for a few minutes before fading away. With no firm scientific explanation, theories abound, many absurd.

I witnessed the lights during my first visit to the area, in the summer of 1992. Camping at *Wiseman's View*, which offers a superb view of the gorge, a light abruptly appeared

near sunset at the bottom of the gorge. We speculated
whether someone had started a large bonfire next to the
Linville River, which flows at the bottom of the gorge. An
actual bonfire at this distance, in this dense, old growth
forest, however. would not have been possible for us to see.
I watched it throughout the night. This 'fire' would change
in intensity, disappear, reappear, then sometimes rise into
the sky before fully disappearing (as if a firework). I recall
it arose from the same area below.

Attempts to witness the lights were made during other
trips, including some to the *Brown Mountain Overlook*,
located several miles away. We saw lights every now and
then, but these could have been any number of things.

Ongoing studies, including that by nearby Appalachian
State University, have yet to conclude the origin or even
explain what exactly is occurring. Some have theorized that
the lights are discharges of static electricity, occurring
under favorable atmospheric conditions. Another is that it
is ball lighting, a rare aerial phenomenon mostly described
as a luminescent, spherical object. Science does not
question its ball lightning's existence, but what exactly it is
… and what causes it … is far from known.

Might we have witnessed ball lightning that night?
Beats me, though the description of ball lightning is mostly
consistent with what we saw. I do recall that throughout the
night we observed a phenomenon called heat lightning
(also called a dry thunderstorm). Thunder is heard,
lightning is seen, just in the absence of clouds and rain.
There are numerous theories of ball lightning, many
involve a relationship with atmospheric conditions
conducive to lightning.

I did take photographs of the phenomenon. At the time, the pictures were hardly interesting. Regretfully, the prints and negatives no longer exist. Today, when I compare my recall of those pictures to the best Google images of the Brown Mountain Lights, mine were far superior. Oh, well.

An uprooted tree teetering over the edge (Babel Tower Trail, Linville Gorge).

CARVER'S GAP

Location: Roan Mountain State Park (near the town of Roan Mountain, Tennessee)

Trees and forest commonly run along the mountain summits of the Appalachian Highlands. In a few cases, however, there are mountain *balds*, areas where wild grasses and stunted plants dominate. These are not areas that were intentionally cleared of timber or had been given over to cattle. These are micro ecosystems that have naturally evolved. The three balds adjacent to Carver's Gap are the best examples. These are: *Round Bald, Jane Bald,* and *Grassy Ridge Bald.* This is one incredible trail, regardless of season or weather conditions.

Roan Mountain is a series of summits located near the border of Tennessee and North Carolina. Carver's Gap lies between two of its summits. There is a parking area and usually quite a bit of activity. The Appalachian Trail comes across the gap, making it is a popular section to hike. Trailheads from the base of the mountain are options. There is even Roan Mountain State Park.

To be honest, Carver's Gap is my go-to place for instant gratification. Outstanding views and alien-like terrain become apparent almost immediately. It is a place to be cordial, as it is heavily trafficked (especially near the parking area; it does soon thin out, the farther you go).

From the parking area, the balds are to the east, but you might notice many people going the opposite way. They are heading into some terrific old growth spruce, fir, and hemlock forest (fortunately, the elevation is too high and cold for the Wooly Adelgid to gain foothold). Roan High Knob is the highest point. It is featureless. More interesting is the Roan High Knob AT Shelter (highest shelter on the Appalachian Trail).

Roan High Knob AT Shelter

For a much more challenging and solitary version of these mountain balds, I recommend a trail known as *19E to Hump Mountain*. The trailhead is on the opposite side of the town of Roan Mountain than the road to Carver's Gap. (The Appalachian Trail connects the two). The ascent to Hump Mountain is at first uneventful but does become rather interesting trek by the time it reaches Little Hump Mountain, then Hump Mountain. In comparison to Round, Jane, and Grassy Ridge, the balds here lack the variety of vegetation but offer a terrific 360° view. Altogether, it is a challenging 12 – 14-mile trek (w/nearly 3000' of ascent).

Compare image taken on Roan Mtn …

… with Little Hump Mtn

Sand Cave + White Rocks

Location: Ewing, Virginia / Kentucky (near the Cumberland Gap)

Sand Cave is not a true cave (by *true cave*, meaning limestone eroded by water), but an incredibly deep wind-carved cavity of sandstone. Sand Cave began as a huge rock (several large, unique outcrops in this area). Over time, wind cut, rounded, and eroded into the bottom of the rock, creating an utterly amazing place. Inside, the stone is intricately designed with patterns and endless shades of color. Photography-wise, it is challenging to fully capture the unique swirls and striations that compose the cave's ceiling. The room itself is well over an acre in size. You will be amazed long before reaching the back wall. Making it an even more impressive formation is the outside area surrounding it. It is a lushness as if out of a movie set. It feels like a lost world. There is even a waterfall flowing down the side of the cave's entrance. Even the sand within the cave is awesome. Since the cave continues to form, footprints are gradually filled. Do, however, walk where others have, not for preservation's sake, but, because walking can be difficult in the deep sand, and it is simply easiest to retrace steps.

There is a trek involved in getting there. From the trailhead (at a well-maintained parking area within *Thomas Walker Civic Park*), the path ascends approximately three miles before there is an option to bear right. Take it (either way gets you to Sand Cave, but taking the right is the better option). It is a steep but short ascent that leads to a fork. To the right is the way to White Rocks. To the left, Sand Cave. Most trekkers come to see Sand Cave and tend to give White Rocks just a quick courtesy visit before turning back to Sand Cave. This is a missed opportunity.

Stepping along a rugged section of White Rocks. Often, the surface is flat, smooth, and seamless. Note the trees, several hundred feet below.

From the road, on the drive to the trailhead, White Rocks is an odd and striking geological feature. It is no less that when standing along its edge. From the trail's summit fork (mentioned in previous paragraph), it's a short leg to some very large and impressive outcrops. There is an obvious path that leads to an impressive vista of the valley below. Many think this is the finale. Incorrect. There is a primitive trail that continues along the edge of the woods, parallel to the barren cliff stone. White Rocks gets its name because it is layered with quartzite, giving it a whiteish and shiny appearance. The ridge extends quite a way and remains remarkably flat-topped.

In all, it is an 8 – 10-mile journey, depending on how much extra one explores, once along the ridge. As with many trails, fitness helps (over 2000 feet of ascent) to enjoy this day.

Profile view of entrance to Sand Cave

Location: Grayson Highlands State Park, near Mount Rogers and Whitetop Mountain, Virginia

Allow me to get several complaints out of the way. There is much to dislike about Grayson Highlands: too many people, too much trail development … too touristry. Google it and you will find it promoting its wild ponies. Tourists gather about these 'wild' ponies, perpetually violating the 'do not feed' requests. The wild ponies are tame enough to eat out of their hands.

The magic of this place begins to occur as one separates from the pack. Once one detaches from these tourists, the connection to the land begins to strengthen and the sheer openness of the countryside overcomes all the fading dislikes. The terrain and vegetation differ from the surrounding mountains. It's as if you're in another place.

Wilburn Ridge, for example, is a recommended and fun ascent. The mixture of boulders and plant life is exquisite. It can withstand a fast-paced ascent (and descent), as the rock is 'sticky,' allowing for maintained balance during aggressive footwork. The Appalachian Trail passes alongside its base, leading to more interesting places, including *Mount Rogers* which, at 5729 feet, is the highest peak in Virginia (Ironically, though surrounded by interesting terrain, Mount Rogers' peak is featureless, unremarkable, and without a decent view).

Nearby to Grayson Highlands is the *Creeper Trail*, as well as the towns of Damascus and Abingdon. These are excellent post-adventure destinations that include eateries, overnight accommodations and even bicycle rentals.

SINKING CREEK CAVE

Location: Greene County, Tennessee (Undisclosed)

Length: > 1 Mile

Tennessee has a *lot* of caves. By some estimates, the state has more caves than any other. These are largely based on estimates, as so many caves remain undocumented on private land. Many landowners prefer the public not knowing of a cave's existence, as it often involves unwelcome attention. Exploration is arrived by permission, often accompanied with an understanding of confidentiality. Such is the case of *Sinking Creek Cave*. This is a significant cave system with a highly active creek that flows in and out of multiple entrances. In return for keeping its location secret, I have been given its unlimited access.

In previous generations, young locals explored its passageways, giving features within it such names as *Devil's Kitchen*, a 100ft, near-vertical drop into a pit and stream, drowned by the sound of unseen raging water, flowing somewhere behind the wall of the pit. As these locals aged-out, few have replaced them. Today's technology has provided entertainment more interesting than exploring caves. One of the last of these aged-out explorers, a gentleman who planned to guide me to a second entrance, recently passed away. Sadly, I will have to find it on my own.

Incredibly pleased with this image, as good cave photography can be difficult.

Cave owners face dilemmas, many with consequences. For example, does one install a gate, protecting it from vandals and trespassers but marring the beauty and mystique of the cave's entrance? Does one leave the entrance in its natural form, increasing the chance of someone becoming lost, injured, and requiring rescue? It is the existential question for Caving itself. The preservation of caves via iron fencing works … but restricts those with the passion to explore.

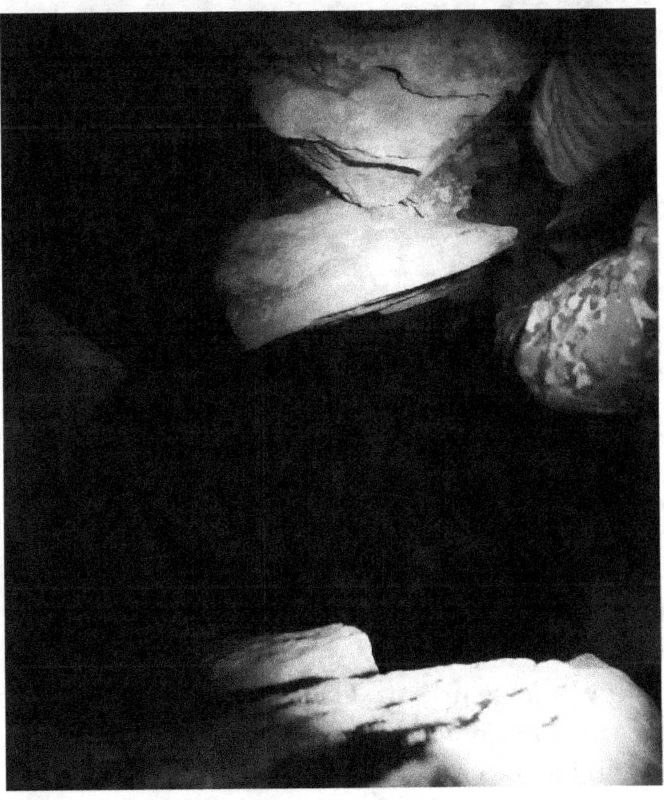

Preparing to free solo the 100' vertical shaft known as "Devil's Kitchen."

Moonshiner's Cave

Location: Greene County, Tennessee (Undisclosed)

Length: >200 Meters

It would be hard to surpass the colorful history and experience in reaching this Greene County, TN hideaway. Locals tell me the cave was briefly used as a Confederate Army's encampment during the Civil War. Then, for decades it was used for family business purposes … to house a moonshining still.

Moonshiner's Cave is located alongside a steep mountainous hollow that it completely hidden from view from those driving along Interstate 81, several miles away. To get there, one must take a winding, paved road that later turns into a narrow, tar & gravel road that … stops. Indeed, one literally drives to the end of the road.

This is a tough rural settlement. Those who live here are left alone and prefer it that way. An unfamiliar vehicle is quickly noticed. The Confederate flag adorns several homes. Dogs stand chained at the entrance of gravel driveways. Problems tend to be handled without law enforcement.

The cave lies on private property a mile beyond the end of the tar road. Its owner does not allow anyone to proceed without permission. Too rough for vehicles, one must trek on foot or via ATV (All-Terrain Vehicle) along a very jagged dirt road that ascends through a series of steep, narrow hollows from which water flows into a creek running parallel to the dirt road. It quickly becomes a no-man's land. Coyotes patrol the area. Commonly during my visits, coyotes stand along the surrounding hills and bark in agitation at my presence. Smart animals, they keep hidden within the trees, allowing me just the occasional glimpse of their movements. Bear tracks and bear scat (poop) are all along the dirt road. Self-explanatory.

Inside the cave entrance, evidence of past moonshining still exists. Deeper, there is little evidence of exploration. It is a true hideout. I mention this place not because you can go there but, even if left to your imagination, so that you know places like it still exist.

WORLEY'S CAVE

Location: 461 Timber Ridge Road, Bluff City, Tennessee

Length: >4 Miles

One of the largest and longest caves in east Tennessee is Worley's Cave. Not commercialized as nearby *Bristol Caverns*, Worley's experiences a steady stream of adventure seekers and is a terrific option for those wanting the accessibility and encounter of a wild cave. Meeting the owner is usually a pleasant experience.

Permission to cave is obtained by stopping at the owner's home and completing a simple registration form (by front door) and paying a small cash fee. From there, it is a short drive to a dirt/gravel parking area. Homemade signage points the way to the cave (just a brief walk).

While self-tours are permissible (by owner's discretion), first-timers should consider a guided tour with one of several local adventure companies (unassociated with the cave's owner). A 'steady stream of adventure seekers' is a relative term, and it is not uncommon for just a couple groups of cavers to be inside at one time. For such a large cave, this means one could easily go an hour or two without encountering others, and it is possible to become disoriented in the meantime. Such experiences can be extremely uncomfortable, even if just for a few moments (By the way, compasses do work inside a cave & most caves generally bear in a single direction). Go with someone familiar with the cave.

Worley's might be best considered as a hybrid between a show cave and a wild cave. A show cave, or commercialized cave, has been altered so that it is accessible and safe for the pubic. By 'altered,' meaning that such features as pathways, lighting, and guided tours have been inserted. Conversely, a wild cave is a place preserved in its natural form. Such places are not for everyone. In fact, such places are for few. The physical aspects are difficult enough. One might be required to squeeze through very tight places, climb, crawl, rappel, slide upon mud, or sink beneath water in absolute darkness. There are no lights along the passages. No handrails. No level pathways. Worley's is heavily trafficked, and, generally, pathways are firm and apparent, but otherwise it is left in its natural state.

There is the main entrance, called the "Dry Mouth" and a smaller entrance from which there is an outflow of a creek, called the "Wet Mouth." This is a walkable water passage that runs parallel to the Dry Mouth (though much shorter in length). Predictably, it is much less traveled … and quite fun.

Ultimately, a cave is a cave, and it befalls each caver to handle the mental aspects of caving. Being within the deep is the mirror image of mountainous heights and maintaining composure with either is unknown until being there. You don't know until you know … and I have witnessed the change of those who were so enthusiastic in experiencing caving, only to succumb to a state so panic stricken that they literally were unable to return and required assistance to the cave's entrance.

Short descent to the 'Wet Mouth' entrance of Worley's Cave

BIG CHERRY LAKE

Location: near Big Stone Gap, Virginia

     Big Cherry Lake (aka Reservoir) is part of a system of mountain lakes and reservoirs that originate from the nearby High Knob area. Best known for fishing, Big Cherry makes my list for other reasons. At 3120 feet elevation, it sits in a basin surrounded by a thick forest. The area is very isolated. Often, I am the only person on the water or even in the area. It is noticeably quiet. Motorized craft are not allowed on the water. Bear, bobcat, deer, and turkey are some of the wildlife commonly residing here. So too beaver, which thrive on the fish. The shallow areas of the lake can be swamp like, with groves of trees growing from beneath the water's surface. Additionally, the shallow waters are filled with an otherworldly aquatic plant called *Hornwort*. Offshoots of the main body of water are narrow waterways. Surrounded by trees and ascents, these waterways create a feeling of traveling through a loch.

It is a fantastic area to practice multiple skills. Often, I set out via kayak but later dock against an accessible bank and begin trekking on foot, typically to reach a chosen location, itself reached by utilizing map and compass, or by having memorized the objective's terrain and location.   Most of the surrounding banks are thickly walled by nearly impenetrable wild mountain laurel. Combined with a maze of fallen trees (mostly because of beaver), it is the ultimate obstacle course. Traveling short distances can take considerable time and energy. Furthermore, due to beaver activity, water flow is often obstructed, creating marshes and pools where water otherwise would not be. Once, I had no alternative but to walk across a beaver dam. Beaver aren't the friendliest creatures; I did not want to fall through into a den, atop a creature capable of chewing down large trees. My concerns were unwarranted, as the dam proved impressively sturdy and allowed me to walk across the water.

It is the experience of paddling the calm waters and silent isolation that makes Big Cherry worthy of adventure.

FRENCH BROAD RIVER

Location: North Carolina / Tennessee

The French Broad River is believed to be among the oldest rivers in the world. Originating near the border of South and North Carolina, it flows through North Carolina and into Tennessee, sharing water with the Pigeon, Nolichucky, Holston, and Tennessee rivers.

Unlike the isolated water of Big Cherry, sections of the French Broad River are commercialized by adventure rafting companies. People and rafts abound. Indeed, for those who never have, whitewater rafting it is well-worth the experience. With a series of Class 2 and 3 rapids, the French Broad River is easy enough for beginners while still offering enough excitement for those experienced.

An enjoyable rafting adventure begins with a bad bus drive up the river. The more cramped the bus, the more terrible the jokes, the curvier the road, the more likely you will have a memorable time. Successful whitewater rafting is to work as a team. This means trusting and obeying the river guide's commands and paddling in synch. Seven to a raft is most often considered full, with two abreast except for the river guide, who sits alone in the rear. Lead rafters must remain attentive, and carefully follow the instructions of the guide, for those behind the two leads tend to visually follow whatever the lead is doing.

A routine tour lasts around an hour on the water, includes a handful of short rapids, and provides enough time to bond with the river. As a personal rule, aboard the raft of the craziest guide you can find. Upon return, remember to tip your guide generously.

For the longest time, I never fell out of a raft. This despite rafting whitewater such as West Virginia's *Gauley River* (which includes Class V rapids). Rafts are constructed so that one's foot can 'dig' into the interior's edge. Usually, it keeps one in the raft … usually. The first time I was washed out, it was no contest. In one instant, I was in the raft. In the next, I was in the river. Water rules. It was a blast.

Whitewater classification range between Class I and Class V (though a Class VI category does exist for extraordinary waters and situations). Class IV and above are the truly hazardous rapids on a river yet, keeping in mind that it is possible to drown in a bathtub, always be safety conscious in and around water.

LITTLE STONY FALLS

Location: Jefferson National Forest (near Dungannon, Virginia)

Little Stony Falls consist of several impressive waterfalls. It is an easy hike with an easier optional parking just above the falls. Here, the trail is graveled and bridges the creek at several strategic places. I have long applauded the efforts by The Commonwealth of Virginia when it comes to parks and trails. Places such as this provide everyone with an opportunity to enjoy impressive nature.

Little Stony National Recreational Trail ascends alongside the photogenic Little Stony Creek that features an abundance of gigantic boulders and deep pools. From the parking area there is the trailhead, and soon to the right, one may observe gated cave entrances. I know virtually nothing of these, but suspect it is a single cave with multiple entrances. That the entrances are gated, and with a not-so-subtle warning signage by the Commonwealth of Virginia to stay out, implies that there are substantial passageways and/or a hibernating bat population.

Not to encourage one to violate cave conservation efforts, but the image above clearly indicates that traffic in and out this entrance can occur.

Nearby is the *High Knob Recreation Area. Bark Camp, Benge's Trail, Flag Rock*, and *High Knob Lookout Tower* are just some of its attractions. Little Stony is located near the small town of Dungannon, Virginia. Exploring small towns such as Dungannon itself can make for an excellent adventure.

Fort Blackmore is nearby, and features what was for the longest time a locally kept secret known as the *Devil's Bathtub*. Now known and heavily trafficked, the trail is becoming dummy-proofed with trail markers and an easier route. As a result, the integrity of the original challenge in finding it is fading, and I disappointingly no longer list the

Devil's Bathtub as a favorite. I will mention that the waterflow here remains undisturbed by people or development. The crystal clarity of the water is considered rare today but would have been common before people began altering the environment.

Me, submerged in Devil's Bathtub … as cold and clear as water gets.

ABRAMS FALLS (VA)

Location: Between Mendota, Virginia and Bristol, VA/TN

Abram's Falls, at approximately 70ft high, is perhaps the most significant privately owned waterfall in the Appalachian Highlands … and it is hardly known. In the 1990s, I would offer to pick up trash in exchange to visit the falls. Nowadays, permission to access the area is granted via online registration. From the parking area (a widened area at the end of the gravel road), it is a short hike (approximately 1 mile) not suitable for everyone. Injuries and sometimes even death occur along the steep trail, slick rocks, and falls.

The largest black bear sighting I have witnessed was at the trailhead of Abrams Falls. My best story, though, was in 2008. As preview to attending that night's premier of *Indiana Jones and the Crystal Skull,* I planned a mini adventure with my eight-year-old son … and in the process, broke several safety rules I knew better than to break. You see, we were originally to go elsewhere but, without alerting any of my family, I switched the destination to Abrams Falls.

Relatively few people have even heard of this waterfall, even less know how to get there. This is an area very remote, on private land, at the time there was no cell phone coverage, the trail was slippery and hazardous. What could possibly go wrong?

All was well until an unprecedented event occurred: I slipped … tumbled … and landed badly. Unconscious for several seconds, I was bruised from left to right, and from head to toe. The top of my head was bleeding profusely. Later, I was diagnosed with a mild concussion and a torn (absolutely pulverized) triceps muscle. I recall being dazed but knowing that a little boy stood, watching me, expecting me to get up. And so, I did get up … and we began slowly walking, not back to the vehicle, but *onward* to the falls. The real-life Indiana Jones was not going to let his son down (and, yes, we did attend the premiere).

Mostly cleaned up … but a little blood still flowing down my forehead.

The best have an uncanny way

To smell what has been there

And taste what is coming

In the silence, they can hear it

And see it in the dark

Able to touch what is missing

Bringing all together

Within it, finding the dance

VALLEY OF THE CAVES

Yellow markers indicate all my area cave finds. *Image by Google Earth

The sacredness of the world is that it never left the light; the sanctity of the cave is that it never left the darkness ~

From earliest memories, I have been strongly interested in fossils, caves, and the Native American. Fortunately, I grew up in an area suited for all three. In an age before the internet, there was no information at my fingertips, no Google. Though plenty of books on Indigenous people and fossils existed, there was much less material available on caves, and I was quite unaware that a significant abundance of caves existed in the region around my home. People knew of caves and explored them. Almost legendary status were Native American burial caves. Accounts of these were rare, and with little collective knowledge. By the 1970's that began to change. The study of caves, *Speleology*, was evolving into a true science. Cavers began organizing and collaborating with *grottos* (organized local caving groups). Preservation efforts arose as, until that time, caves were subject to intentional damage with little repercussion. As the Commonwealth of Virginia recognized this, preservation efforts began in the attempt to prevent looters and vandals from causing further damage and, in 1979, passed sweeping cave conservation legislation. Speleology was coming of age.

Valley of the Caves is an informal name I use to describe Powell Valley, Virginia. North of the valley is Stone Mountain. To the south, Powell Mountain. The hallmark of Powell Mountain is a very distinct line of vertical limestone cliffs. Called *Greenbrier Limestone*, this stone is the perfect composition and age for cave development. Limestone is sedimentary rock, formed as layers and layers of mud build and compress. These are not thin layers. Greenbrier Limestone can be 300 feet thick. Furthermore, layers below (older rock) and layers above (younger) have different compositions and characteristics. The Greenbrier Limestone that runs along Powell Mountain, from Norton to Duffield, Virginia is where I like to look. To 'like' looking there is a bit twisted for, in hopes of finding something forgotten or undiscovered, I trek to places most difficult in accessibility. The section of Powell Mountain closest to our home was most prominent and with the most dramatic outcrops of limestone. As picturesque as these cliffs are, weatherization constantly occurs, breaking at the weakest points. Below these cliffs, fallen rocks, many larger than vehicles, litter the ground. When a large rock falls from the cliffs, it lands on very steep terrain, and begins to roll down, leaving in places a line of trees knocked aside from the wake of its path. I have been nearby during the thunderous moments of rock fall, and it is not pleasant. Falling rock is not the only potential hazard. Landslides can occur, especially if the mountain becomes oversaturated, creating a raging stream of mud and earth. The energy of this must be incredible, as I have seen areas a couple acres in size swept clean. Below it, gigantic mounds of stone, dirt, and uprooted trees. A person would not want to be the inadvertent trigger of such an event.

Powell Valley belongs to Wise County, Virginia. Coal mining country. To the casual observer, much of the area might seem useless. At any given direction, one was surrounded by deep gullies, steep gaps, and sheer mountainsides. Roads constantly curved to follow the contour of the terrain. Other than hunters, few ventured into woods.

Rocky Hollow Cave and *Kelly Cave* were the largest known caves in the area until the discovery of what is now known as the *Omega Cave System*. As luck would have it, Omega's main entrance lies just outside the farthest reaches of my boyhood explorations of Powell Mountain. By the time my travels expanded, Omega was already known. This is no bittersweet tail; several of my discoveries are likely to be connecting offshoots of Omega.

Caves had long been misunderstood. Many kept shrouded in secrecy. Landowners learned to be wary of those entering caves on their property. They could become lost, injured, or paint graffiti inside the cave. Animals, such as cows, might wander or stumble in, prompting some to destroy or fill in an entrance. Today, though vandalism continues to be a concern (a bit less so, with many of the significant caves now installed with cave gates), a new problem has superseded it: the disturbance of hibernating bats compounded by the spread of White Nose Syndrome (as cavers themselves can unintentionally spread by means of contaminated gear).

What I'm getting at is that there is no red carpet awaiting you at the cave's entrance. To search for caves is to do so without much assistance. Then, considerations must be made for the cave itself (ex. Waiting for bats to come out of hibernation). It would be an improbable quest to list all the caves I have entered. As a result, **BEEN** describes only the caves I have found on my own, via exploration, skill … and luck around the eastern rim of Powell Valley.

What counts as a cave? There's a little judgment calling involved but, generally, it's an opening in the rock at least 20 feet in length and possessing enough characteristics of a cave (for example, not a random crack in the stone, but a cavity carved out by water). Some are so extensive that teams are required (and significant time) to tediously map. More often, one finds endless pockmarked crags and crevasses of 'almost-caves' (a feature that just doesn't meet criteria). Overhangs, for example, even those used as encampments are great shelters but are not caves. Some of what I count as caves are borderline. Some that I didn't count are also borderline.

Recently, I found a small cavity tunneling into the mountainside. It had every feature of a cave, yet it narrowed so quickly that a person could barely fit before stoppage. I was torn but could not count it as a cave find. Even then, I break this rule once and hit a borderline on another with the following list of twenty-one area caves.

Most of my cave finds on Powell Mountain are at an average elevation of 2700 feet or at whatever elevation the line of exposed limestone cliffs happens to be. There are more elevation variations of cave locations on Stone Mountain.

Standing inside the perimeter of a landslide … earth, stone, and trees swept away.

Apologies with using both English and Metric Systems. Depending on the subject, I use one or the other (for example, I sprint in meters but run by miles … go figure). In keeping with the informalities of the book, I will continue using both. Now, let us move on to the caves …

Location: Powell Valley, 36°53'46.67" N   82°40'48.38" W

Elevation: 1724 Feet

Length: 20 Feet

Description: Located on an otherwise geologically featureless hillside, a small outcrop of rock included a narrow opening that tunneled downward for approximately 20'.

This cave no longer exists, having partially collapsed by the time of my last visit, sometime in the 1980's. I intend to go back to determine if it was even a true cave or, more likely, an unusual hillside cavity. Regardless, it was one's first discovery (eight-year-old at the time). A place captivating, compelling, … setting the stage for a lifetime of discovery.

Most caves are formed in limestone. Imagine rainwater falling on a mountain. Water seeps through the leaves and soil before sinking into the ground, becoming slightly acidic by this point. Into cracks and crevasses, this slightly acidic water begins to slowly eat away at the limestone. What begins as a crack becomes a cavity. The cavity lengthens. Ultimately, a cave system forms. Many caves feature formations, such as stalactites and stalagmites.

Here is a thought: as far as land is concerned, just about all the world has been explored. As far as the oceans are concerned, we've mapped much of it. With the subterranean domain, however, we have hardly tapped into it, and it is very much possible to go where no one has gone before. At the time of this writing, an explorer does not have to be a deep-sea diver, an astronaut, nor the first person on Mars. The explorer is that persistent, systematic, determined caver who dares enter the abyss.

Location: Powell Valley, 36°53'42.78" N   82°41'00.03" W

Elevation: 1650 Feet

Length: Unknown (continues)

Description: Single, horizontal passage tunnelling into the hillside. A small stream flows out its entrance. Length of cave is unknown (that there is no nearby surface source of the stream that flows from its entrance, its length is potentially substantial). It continues beyond the few feet I penetrated.

I knew of this cave by 1976. This cave is adjacent and faces perpendicular to a creek known as *Butcher's Fork*. From the entrance there flows a small stream. This is the only Powell Valley caves I have found that sits on the valley floor. Its potential significance is the source of its stream.

It is a wet crawl to enter, and doable for only a few feet before collapsed stone, probably related to an adjacent hillside depression, impedes further progress.

For years, I frequently visited this site, albeit not to cave. Next to it was an eroding embankment from which one could find small clumps of quartz and sea fossils.

Life is not to elude adversity, but to embrace it. When challenge clinches hold of you, surprise it and grab back!

CAVE III

Location: Powell Mountain, 36°53'03.63" N 82°39'57.08" W

Elevation: 2905 Feet

Length: Unknown (continues)

Description: Single tunnel that begins as a crawl and later develops into a vadose canyon at least 15 meters high (there I go converting from English to Metric).

The 1995 discovery of this cave was based on a false memory that I still recall: crossing the woodlands below, I could see above me a cave entrance at the bottom of the prominent vertical cliffs. A tough 100-meter ascent from where I stood, intense winds signaled an oncoming storm, prompting me to hurry home. It would be another year before returning to that vantage point. With a very determined crawl up the mountain, I reached the cliffs just a few meters to the right of the cave. Just where I knew it was … except the cave's entrance is completely hidden until one practically reaches it. I couldn't have seen the cave from where my memory suggest.

Initially, the cave is unremarkable until, further in, it becomes intricately carved with formations, shaping itself as a narrow passage called a Vadose Canyon. A tight squeeze above, below, and forward, this cave continues.

Closer to the entrance, at least one marine fossil protrudes from the left side wall. Many are confused to why mountain tops hold sea-bottom creatures. The mountains of the Appalachians have long-since eroded; today's mountain 'tops' are but the most stubborn limestone to erode. Valleys have eroded quicker, giving the illusion that the knubs are mountains. Indeed, the highest peak here was once the floor of an ancient seabed.

Location: Powell Mountain, 36°54'29.24" N 82°39'23.51" W

Elevation: 2450 Feet

Length: 150 Feet

Description: Featureless, roomy, mostly horizontal.

My parents called this cave *Saltpetre Cave* (also spelled as *Saltpeter*), and most likely it was used to obtain saltpetre. My mentor, Roy D. Powers Jr., was confused when I inquired if he knew of this cave. Saltpetre caves aren't necessarily named *Saltpetre Cave*, and he was unaware of such a named cave in that proximity. If there is another name for this cave, I do not know it.

In the mid-1970's, my family and I set out on a trek to visit this cave. Included was my brother, Brad, who soon thereafter began what resulted in a very successful golfing career. Along with our parents, themselves busy people, this proved to be our single, significant family trek. Though it proved unsuccessful (we did not locate the cave), we did hike from the sharp curve where today a rock quarry operation is located, all the way to Beaverdam Gap, from which we descended to the Lonesome Pine Country Club. Reflecting, it was a rather impressive accomplishment.

It was 20 years later, in 1996, that I determinedly and successfully located this cave.

Just about any cave that houses bats is a potential saltpetre cave. During the Civil War, the South, short on gunpowder, needed massive quantities of nitrogen so that it could make its own. As it turned out, saltpetre is nitrogen-rich. What I'm trying to avoid telling you is that saltpetre is essentially a combination of bat poop (In caving terminology, it's called *guano*) and pee. Basically, bats eat a ton of bugs each night then go back to the cave and relieve themselves before a good day's rest, over time, building great deposits of nitrogen along the floor of caves. To mine saltpetre was as simple as shoveling s%t (expletive), hauling it out, and extracting the nitrogen.

CAVE V

Location: Powell Mountain 36°54'47.28" N 82°39'36.77" W

Elevation 2307 feet

Length: 60 Feet

Description: Brief crawl leads to a single, level, open room.

Despite belonging to an impressive cliff face, a well-formed and complex entrance, and a well-developed bulbous room, this cave … stops. The entrance also serves as an overhang (with a terrific view of the valley), located a stone's throw above the winding road of Route 610. It is also precariously close to the rock quarry. For all the old tv shows of cave-ins, this one has survived intact the many explosive, ground-shaking blasts of the quarry.

View from the passage leading inside

Initially, I thought this a second entrance, but no passage here

CAVE VI

*Image by Google Earth

Location: Beaverdam Gap, Powell Mountain

36°52'45.50" N 82°40'00.56" W

Elevation: 3144 feet

Length: Unknown

Description: A small, easily overlooked opening. Length: >15 vertical feet that likely continues (due to strong water vapor escape).

This discovery of this entrance occurred by being at the right place at the right time. The right place was a right-sided ascent of Beaverdam Gap. The right time was a wintertime, cold sunrise on a noticeably clear morning. Facing east on my ascent, the sun rose directly in front of me, its rays almost blinding as it reflected off the snow yet it revealed the strong escape of water vapor, also in front of me. It was a small opening in a slightly recessed area of ground, absent of any surrounding outcrop.

Water vapor and air flow are indicative of substantial tunneling. The vertical entrance appeared to have enough hand and foothold to descend without rope, but I elected not to enter without better preparation. Unfortunately, I have not successfully relocated this cave. The diameter of the entrance is approximately 3' and is concealed unless literally standing above it. Possibly, it is connected to Cave 16, itself with profound air flow, as Cave 6 is situated somewhere above.

Undoubtedly, a number of small openings like this exist. I find similar ones, but with diameters too small to count as cave finds. Some of this is due to Powell Mountain's unique cave formation. Normally, when it rains atop a mountain, water sinks and works its way through the rock and eventually shoots its way out through well-developed valley springs, or lower-elevated caves. These are rare on Powell Mountain because beneath the Greenbrier Limestone the underlying rock is very watertight. Other than a crack or weak spots (such as hollows and gaps) on the mountain, drainage water has nowhere to go. Therefore, I find cliffside caves and not valley caves. Internally, the upper half of the mountain is pockmarked, with pools of water with nowhere to go.

I witnessed this one day, standing along the edge of the massive rock quarry that sits at the very edge of the valley. The side of the mountain had been sheered, giving me a look of what was inside … perhaps 200 feet of vertical limestone guts. Several cavities were noted. Caves with no entrances. From a couple, water poured.

CAVE VII: ROCKY HOLLOW PIT

Location: Rocky Hollow, Powell Mountain

36°53'57.43" N 82°39'12.58" W

Elevation: 2974 Feet

Length: 100 Feet

Description: The entrance of this pit cave is an ominous, vertical drop. Line of sight is approximately 30 feet.

Rocky Hollow Pit is a vertical cave (aka Pit Cave) that connects to Rocky Hollow Cave. It is easily seen from an old manway, remarkably close to the edge of the Jefferson National Forest.

Somewhere down this vertical shaft lies a GoPro (aka 'action camera', or 'hands-free video camera') of mine. Alone and safety conscious on a particular trek (my wife states that she will hurt me, should I get injured or killed while on an outing), I decided to tie my helmet and light to a long rope and lower it into the cave. Also attached was my GoPro, which would video the scene. Clever idea, right? Things were going as planned until near the end of raising the rope. Just beyond the line of sight, my helmet became snagged. After several as-gentle-as-possible attempts to tug and undo the snag, I pulled the helmet free … minus the GoPro.

CAVE VIII

Location: Sheep Gap, Powell Mountain

36°52'23.01" N 82°40'54.67" W

Elevation: 2700 Feet

Length: 60 Feet

Description: The entrance has a scalene triangle shape that opens into a single, circular room, extending into the mountain for approximately 60 feet.

Cave 8 would make a for a functional encampment. Level, with ample room to stand upright. Small stones liter the floor. The entrance is located above and along a hazardous cliff line. I accidently dropped a cell phone here once. I joke that it is still falling down the side of the mountain. Such areas as this provide prominent views of the valley below.

This cave is inactive, produces no draft, and is subject to cold temperatures. Notwithstanding, I have

observed an occasional bat hibernating in this cave and, as
a result, leave the cave alone in the winter.

Very steep here. One more step back, and I would have tumbled down the mountain.

The plight of the bat population is due to a fungus
known as *White Nose Syndrome*. Over 90% of the area bat
population has died because of it. Whereas recently as a
decade or two ago, bats were commonplace to watch in the
late-evening sky, today these same skies are empty (much
to the relief of mosquitos, a favorite food of bats). The
surviving population has a long way to go in rebuilding.
People should avoid disturbing hibernating bats, as this
compounds the issue.

CAVE IX

Location: Sheep Gap, Powell Mountain

36°52'22.99" N 82°40'54.67" W

Elevation: 2705 Feet

Length: 30 Feet

Description: Elevated entrance along a cliff. A short, level squeeze opens into a vertical drop consisting of one 30' x 30' room

The tight entrance to this unnamed pit cave quickly leads to a smooth-walled, vertical descent. Below is a circular, single room. I have observed at times moisture at the wall opposite the entrance. It is an intriguing site. The pic below provides a good perspective of what I mean by 'cliffside cave.' This cave is scheduled for descent and exploration in 2022.

Talk about a cliffside entrance!

Cave X

Location: Sheep Gap, Powell Mountain

36°52'22.83" N 82°40'51.41" W

Elevation: 2740 Feet

Length: Unknown (continues)

Description: Single, narrow tunnel. Briefly widens near the entrance.

Located at Sheep Gap, this cave potentially connects with the Omega Cave System. Accessing the entrance requires a crawl, briefly widening before continuing into the mountain as a single, tight passage.

Sheep Gap and Beaverdam Gap are mentioned several times in this journal. Gaps are narrow openings between mountain peaks and ridges. The cliffs of Powell Mountain are so steep that gaps are the most reliable means in successful ascent. Gaps are dry drainage that activate during heavy rains. These are ever-changing places because rocks and trees of various size fall into them and are gradually swept down the mountain as storms briefly transform gaps into raging creeks. With stone and debris atop any stable rock, gaps can make for tricky footwork, and the successful know how to shift one's bodyweight to reduce the chance of falling.

A connecting tunnel to Omega? Further exploration will answer.

Gaps are rough places

Cave XI

Location: Sheep Gap, Powell Mountain

36°52'22.51" N 82°40'47.33" W

Elevation: 2720 Feet

Length: 25 Feet

Description: Single, narrow tunnel that quickly peters out

This cave is located on the eastern side of Sheep Gap, facing into the gap. Not much to report here. A single passage that narrows quickly. The entrance as seen in the above image is as wide as it gets.

The cliffs of Powell Mountain are pocked with small cavities. These appear as contrasting, dark spots upon the white and grey rock. Often, what appears as an entrance is just a trick of the light and angle.

CAVE XII: ROCKY HOLLOW CAVE

Location: Rocky Hollow, Powell Mountain

36°53'56.21" N 82°39'16.12" W

Elevation: 2718 Feet

Length: >1 mile

Description: The wide entrance is iron-fenced w/no access, as this is a protected and dangerous cave with a compelling history.

Rocky Hollow is the largest area cave (excluding Omega Cave System). There is no less than a very compelling history concerning this now-gated cave. Several decades ago, it housed one of the greatest densities of bat population ever observed. This population was already in decline before White Nose Syndrome, at least partially due to disturbances caused by cavers, resulting in Virginia's preservation efforts. I'm told by State officials that the cave still hosts a few hundred federally endangered Indiana bats, as well as several other species in smaller numbers. Rocky Hollow was once a challenging and attractive place to explore. It contains over a mile of passages that include gigantic rooms and multiple 100ft. drops.

Located on an extremely steep section of mountain, it takes a determined grit just to reach it. I found it by deducing that Rocky Hollow Pit might have another entrance down the mountain. Finding it was thrilling. Finding that it had large iron bars drilled into its stone wielded into it was mysterious and impressive, given the logistics that must have been involved (for example, there is no nearby road nor obvious means in transporting material to the site). I spent a bit of time investigating its origins. Turns out that my old mentor, Roy D. Powers, Jr. orchestrated the design and feat of installing the long beams of the iron fencing. Helicopters were used to lower materials. It took a team several days to complete the task. It was truly a legendary accomplishment.

Among iron and stone.

Cave signage just inside Rocky Hollow Cave. Numerous caves are undergoing a similar moratorium in effort to protect endangered bats.

In case you are wondering, trespassing in this Virginia cave is a Class I Misdemeanor. Don't do it. There are many legal options to explore caves. Should you have a local grotto, contact them, or attend their next meeting. Typically, a grotto has the best area knowledge of caves.

Cave XIII

Location: Powell Mountain 36°54'11.49" N 82°39'11.51"W

Elevation: 2762 Feet

Length: 30 Feet

Description: The entrance and single, cramped passage is ragged, old, and ugly.

Adjacent to the Jefferson National Forest boundary, hidden from view of an overpassing old manway. Overlooks a steep, rugged hollow. Not much else to say.

Cave XIV

Location: Powell Mountain

36°54'04.49" N 82°39'12.53" W

Elevation: 2681 Feet

Length: 40 Feet

Description: A striking pointed entrance. Level, single, tunneling passage that quickly angles up into the mountain.

The area surrounding this cave is prime for cave. It has been a surprise and disappointment in not having found any significant caves here.

Location: Beaverdam Gap, Powell Mountain

36°52'50.31" N 82°40'08.61" W

Elevation:2733

Length: 20 Feet

Description: Single, level tunnel

This is a tubular, straight tunnel one may enter for a few feet before narrowing. Though being generous with length, it possesses enough cave characteristics to qualify.

CAVE XVI

Location: Beaverdam Gap, Powell Mountain

36°52'49.01" N 82°40'05.95" W

Elevation: 2865 Feet

Length: Unknown (continues)

Description: Large, single, level tunnel leads to a brief crawl before things get complicated.

This is a significant cave, potentially rivaling Rocky Hollow Cave in size. Located at the top line of the outcrops of Beaverdam Gap, I found this cave during an ascent (much easier accessing the cave from above). The significance of this cave is evidenced by a strong airflow venting from its dramatic, horizontal tunnel-like entrance. Despite the dramatic entrance and large initial tunnel, this cave quickly gets complicated with narrow, twisting, descending passage.

I've discussed this cave with prominent caver, Mike Ficco, an international cave exploring specialist who also independently found this cave. Mike is credited as a discoverer of the Omega Cave System. With this cave, it continued beyond his tedious and best efforts.

Location: Stone Mountain

36°53'41.84" N 82°43'13.09" W

Elevation: 2277 Feet

Length: Visible for 30 Feet (continues?)

Description: Single, narrow, 45° descending tunnel at least 30ft. in length. Looks climbable via hands/feet.

This is one of those unexpected, lucky cave finds. The entrance is small and not part of any visibly significant bedrock. It is a recent find and plans for exploration are evolving. It appears climbable with perhaps modest rope assist; the question is 'does it open up or narrow?'

Does it open or narrow?

This side of Stone Mountain faces southward, and it has a more stunted, tighter terrain than the northward-facing Powell Mountain. Saplings and squat foliage are thick. Outcrops of stone are haphazard and seemingly everywhere (in contrast to the distinct cliffs and outcrops of Powell Mountain). Hmm, maybe that's why they named it *Stone Mountain*.

CAVE XVIII

Location: Stone Mountain

36°54'20.33" N 82°43'16.90" W

Elevation: 3012 Feet

Length: 25 Feet

Description: Single, low dome room.

I found this cave after ascending Stone Mountain and continuing northward, in the general direction of the town of Appalachia. This is no-man's land within this section of the Jefferson National Forest (Clinch Ranger District). The area surrounding this cave is extremely dense with laurel, so effectively concealing the entrance from view that one must crawl to the edge then skim along the unusually straight lined 25ft high outcrop just to observe it.

This exposed limestone is interesting to study via satellite, no less interesting to view in person, and deserves further exploration. I followed an old, dirt road, very much overgrown with laurel. For those unfamiliar with gnarly Mountain Laurel, it is absolutely to be avoided where dense, for it is extremely frustrating and difficult to cross (I'm a believer in the tales of those early settlers being driven mad by laurel).

Coyote scat is often observed around here, and I did recently happen across a black bear' humerus bone (searched but couldn't find any other bones). Thick and heavy, I made it into a nice flint-head axe.

From finding a bear bone to making it into an axe

CAVE XIX: ELF GLEN

Location: Stone Mountain

36°53'58.95" N 82°42'49.08" W

Elevation: 2030 Feet

Length: 40 Feet

Description: 15' drop leads to a short, level passage w/surprisingly well-developed formations.

Elf Glen overlooks a narrow gap, camouflaged within a countless maze of identical looking boulders and ragged outcrops. Indeed, one could be within just a few feet of the entrance and never know it.

The vertical entrance of Elf Glen is impressive. There is no indication of what awaits inside its blackened void. I vividly recall the excitement of first entry, just moments after finding it while on a typical solo exploration. After the initial climb down, I began walking through a single, level passage that … abruptly ended. Indeed, the entrance is the most impressive feature of this short cave, though the formations inside are surprisingly detailed.

In an incredible coincidence, Elf Glen is the site where I met Mike Ficco and his wife, Katarina Kosic Ficco, herself a professional caver. Mike is credited as the discoverer of Omega Cave. Katarina is well-known in her own right. They are the ones who named this cave *Elf Glen*.

Nice formations for such a short cave

CAVE XX: KELLY DISAPPOINTMENT

Location: Stone Mountain

36°53'58.95" N 82°42'40.08" W

Elevation: 2118 Feet

Length: >50 Feet

Description: Low and wide. Entrance has commanding view of gap and valley.

Not sure if this is its official name, but I wonder how many people have climbed to *Kelly Disappointment* thinking they had found Kelly Cave. This cave, so-named by Katarina Kosic Ficco, *is* close to Kelly Cave, but close is no guarantee of finding anything in these parts. The nearby Kelly Cave is an exceedingly difficult entrance to locate. Kelly Disappointment becomes observable once one has progressed far enough up a very rugged gap. Much to one's disappointment, however, one quickly discovers that it is not Kelly Cave. It is a strong entrance, and promising crawl, but the passage soon halts. Thus, its name, Kelly Disappointment.

For every protected cave, numerous entrances are not gated. This is a testament to the number of caves in the region. My caving mentor, Roy D. Powers Jr., an engineer, and college instructor, designed the first successful cave gates ('gated' and 'fenced' are often interchangeable terms, though a gated caves implies an access). For decades, he dedicated most of his spare time to the preservation of caves by installing his designed gates.

Obviously, permission must be granted to explore a gated cave. This can often be accomplished by joining or participating with a local caving grotto (club).

CAVE XXI: KELLY CAVE

Location: Stone Mountain (*Due to an agreement and preservation efforts, I am bound to confidentiality of this site's location)

Elevation: Confidential

Length: > 1 Mile

Description: With an entrance all but hidden from view, it is a double-gated, complex caves that includes a waterfall, lake, twisting passages and gym-sized rooms.

Kelly Cave is a legendary beast of a cave. Ironically, fewer people know of its existence than with previous generations. Expansive, complex, lengthy and possibly not fully explored by any living person, Kelly Cave features include a gymnasium sized room, numerous offshoot passages, a roaring waterfall, a lake, and vertical passages. Heavily vandalized and stripped of most natural formations, for generations it was a go-to place for local adventurers. Even my maternal grandmother (as opposite an adventurer as one can be) visited this cave during the late-1920s. Currently, Kelly Cave is no less than double-gated, largely due to an effort to protect the vulnerable bat population.

Double-trouble: Kelly Cave's entrance iron fencing.

Location: To be determined

Elevation: To be determined

Distance: To be determined

Description: To be determined

With continued effort and methodical search, I am optimistic that there will be a 22nd area cave find. Already, I am planning to extend exploration further southwest along Powell Mountain. This area of new search begins just southwest of Cracker's Neck and will continue to an area known as Jasper (near Duffield). The Jefferson National Forest area adjacent to the town of Appalachia is another area of interest.

Finding a cave is an overly exciting moment, especially when a cave is in an area predetermined as having good potential. A good practice in searching for caves is to study maps and, better yet, satellite imagery such as Google Earth. Caves serves as nature's gutter system. Especially with mountains, caves are essential in draining water. Often, what you are looking for lies not only in geology, but in hydrology. Look at a mountain three-dimensionally, and search for sunken regions. Often, these are markers of water movement and drainage beneath. I've had great success predicting where caves should be, based on this single strategy.

FOSSILS + POINTS

Various fossils of sea dwelling creatures

Location: Appalachian Highlands

Limestone rock are layers of seabed debris. Around 300 million years ago, the sea creatures of what is now Powell Valley would become part of this debris. A small percentage became fossilized. Today, by means of weathering, erosion, or digging, these fossils reach the surface. Not to be confused with dinosaur bones, these are much older and include such creatures such as crinoids, mollusks, and sponges.

Adjacent to our Virginia home were fields and cow pasturelands. The weight and hooves of these animals are such that they erode ground cover. The cows often congregated at certain areas, these were usually places to cross steams, drink, or to find shade. Heavy ground damage and embankment erosion were common. There were two nearby areas in particular that yielded consistent fossil finds. (Undoubtedly, there are many more areas, the entire valley consists of the same aged limestone, these were just the ones I used.).

As the decades past by, the landowner finally retired, the cows went away, and the pasturelands began to heal and transform back into woodlands. Without the constant traffic of cows, my two best areas of erosion closed, effectively sealing away the easy finds of exposed fossils.

Crinoids. Found near Clinch Mountain (Rosedale, VA.)

With the best fossil finds many years past, I believed that chapter of my life to be ended. It has been recent, however, that we found impressive fossils during a trek to *The Great Channels*, near Rosedale, Virginia. Coming in from *Brumley Mountain Trail* we observed that many of the lighter colored rocks contained large crinoids.

Fossil hunting is like searching for arrowheads, rocks, and minerals: it's a matter of training the eye to see certain shapes, sizes, and/or colors. At my best, I could *see* a fossil even when it was face-down on the ground.

Concerning arrowheads: a more appropriate term than arrowheads is *points*. This is a broader term that incudes spear points, arrowheads, scrapers, and axe heads. Limestone doesn't make good points. Quartz (including flint, jasper, quartzite), however, makes great points, and most everything one might find in the Appalachian Highlands originates from the quartz-rich western-North Carolina mountains. Places like *Shiny Rock* (a North Carolina peak) were something akin to manufacturing hubs of Native American weapons and tools.

Historically, at least, or so I am told, the Fort Blackmore (near the Clinch River) area yielded more Indigenous artifacts than any other area in the Appalachian Highlands. My understanding is that the Cherokee Indians were the last tribe to control the area. With their stronghold in the western North Carolina mountains, the Cherokee extended into southwest Virginia during certain seasons. Base and transient camps typically were strategically located adjacent to sources of water. That is why the best places in the valleys to search and find artifacts is along the creeks, riverbanks, and to walk the freshly plowed fields (usually level ground and often adjacent to water). A feature common in these settings is known as an *Indian Mound*. These mounds were deliberate constructions, often related to burials and rituals. In the mountainous areas overlooking the valleys, overhangs and cave entrances were commonly used as base or transient camps. Large caves were especially convenient, as caves maintain a year-round temperature in the low 50s (providing cool in the summer, warm in the winter). There is little evidence of mounds in these areas. Instead, there was the utilization of caves as burial sites (not exclusive, as a cave on the valley floor might easily be chosen as a burial site). Only several dozen caves in the region are known burial caves. It is highly likely, however, that many more burial cave sites once existed.

Points (aka: arrowheads)

There were few resources in past decades to preserve caves and any artifacts within them. Searching for and removing these relics were mostly legal up until 1979, when State and Federal Laws were enacted and began restricting the disturbance, removal, etc. of items ranging from cave formations to Native American remains.

Prior to 1979, stewardship did not necessarily conflict with unearthing artifacts, even for those who understood that important knowledge would be lost in the process. Good people sought to extract artifacts as a means of saving them. Prior to 1979 there were few regulations, and few means in protecting sensitive sites. Barely 100 years after the forced displacement of the local Native Americans, evidence of their culture had increasingly become perishable. It was a lose-lose prospect for those who would otherwise prefer leaving still-preserved sites alone. Discovered sites would be excavated, regardless. Indeed, for artifact hunters, it was always open season. From their perspective, the heirs to these Native Americans were long since displaced. It was considered fair game. It was the challenge and excitement of the find. These artifacts were like treasure hunting, yet not to sell, but to be collected. If you found something and didn't' take it, someone else likely would.

Such was the experience of my maternal grandfather, who had long been a backwoods explorer and amateur scientist. His interests ranged widely, from botany to geology, from wildlife to Native Americans. In the 1950s, he became aware of a Native American burial cave in Dickenson County(?), Virginia. I know of this because it just so happened that he took one of his young daughters to this site, and she happens to be my mother. What follows is an interesting tale:

Pre-dating interstate highways, or even large roads, the drive alone would have been an adventuresome rural journey. The cave was a pit cave (vertical) in a remote field and its entrance very small, perhaps three feet in width. My mother recalls being lowered approximately 15-20' by rope, then accompanied by her father and several of his compatriots. She described the vertical shaft as being tight, and that initially the cave was cramped, but that after crawling through a narrow, level passage, it opened into a room perhaps 20' in diameter and high enough so that one could fully stand. In the center of the room was what appeared to be a mound of dirt, approximately mid-thigh in height. Water dripping from above had washed away a section of this 'dirt,' and there they could see exposed skeletal remains of what they later estimated were several people. When they resurfaced from the cave, they did so with a human skull.

Later, as any good student might do, my mother obtained her father's permissions to take the skull to school, to show it to her science teacher. Unfortunately, that day the teacher dropped and shattered the skull. Surely, it was a mortifying moment. Returning home with a bag of fragments, my mother dreaded telling her father, but when she told him, to her surprise, after a deep breath and a moment's pause, all he said was "Things happen." Good man! This tragic tale doesn't end there. Years later, when I learned that the fragments had been placed in a bag, there was that moment of hope and excitement. Fragments could be reconstructed. Might the skull have been stored away? I was told, however, that my grandmother, not understanding the significance of the broken treasure, had long ago thrown away the bag and fragments.

The account is a rare description of a burial cave. Far from simply being dropped into the pit, the bodies had been intentionally lowered, then taken through the narrow passage and specifically placed into the center of the room. Any similar process would have required planning and effort, but with the cave in absolute darkness, those who buried these remains would have also used torches. Just imagine.

Today, interest and the hunt for Native American artifacts has again grown intense, and seems mostly fueled by money, as there is an international market for it. YouTube videos show where to search and how to find. There is even a cable series glamorizing those who hunt for artifacts. It reminds me of the change of spirit that occurred in the 1990s with sports cards. Prior to that, cards were collected and traded for fun by kids (remember, prior to the sports cards craze that began in the 1990s, baseball cards had no monetary value … other than a Ruth or Mantle). Then, as cards became investments and judged almost solely by value, the fun vanished.

The Native American artifact hunters I knew as a kid had aged-out of searching the fields, but they still showed off their collections with the fun spirit of a child, and with no thought nor interest in selling. I do not know if there was even much of a market for artifacts back then. Greed has corrupted. None of my points are for sale.

THE RANGER

Adventure itself prefers to remain dormant, featureless, and nameless; it is the adventurer who must awaken adventure, embody it, and remind it its name ~

Several years ago, I formed a group known as CAMEL Team. *CAMEL* is acronym for **CA**ves **M**ountains **EL**ements. CAMEL Team is a group and concept that embodies the spirit of challenge, adventure, and exploration. There are two divisions: *Tactical & Combatives*, and *Caving & Mountaineering*. Both incorporate the idealized *Ranger* and train accordingly. The ranger is one capable of navigating through any type of challenging encounter, situation, condition, or terrain. A key concept is the ranger immerses him/herself into the environment. Fully explored and described in my book, *The Codex Bellum: Iron Wrapped In Cotton* (albeit I use the term 'warrior' instead of 'ranger'), the following are several key concepts, especially when applied to exploring the rugged environment:

- **Answer your inner, often insensible calling** .. the journey begins with the willingness to abandon familiarity and step into the unknown …We all share the challenge to enter the abyss, tame our demons, discover our power, and return with the light
- **Cut your own groove** … action does not get one there, action *is* the place … Visualization and actualization are one's map and machete; explore possibility, carve opportunity, and forge a trail of success
- **Explore your story** … where you step into transformation, there is your answer … Learn to fall and stand, for these are instances of truth … Use defeat, for it can be the greatest teacher, and the most valuable tools are often reshaped mistakes
- **Enrich your story** by adding characters … companions … Share the experience … Inheritance isn't what you get, but what you give
- **Be changed** … Challenge, adventure, and exploration are voyages of clumsiness, roughness, and humility … delivering one towards skill, eloquence and a fierceness of body, spirit, and mind

Own what you are starting

Be absorbed into the environment

Awaken all your senses

Consider everything animate and be open to dialogue

Embrace awe and be whelmed

Navigate uncertainty

Alter your course to follow a question

Trace things back to its root

With deep breaths, feel the stillness

Notice colors, geometry, and movements

Understand these are telling stories

Think with clarity, rest in providence

Discover the rhythm of your dance

Return, indescribably changed

For you have finished what you started ~

Explorations, challenges, and adventures are not always tangible places, nor events. Experiencing the moment doesn't occur via one's camera lens. The ultimate journey, perhaps, is within oneself, the most valued skill intangible, and the greatest experience something mysterious or unseen. Can you become higher than the obstacle or deeper than the unknown? Can you become longer than the separation or tougher than the problem? Can you succeed despite failure? Can you remain balanced, centered, even in disarray?

In the process of reaching for the top,

do not overlook uniting with the mountain ~

Exploration is not a place; it is a mindset. To be an explorer doesn't require you to travel to some phenomenal location. It can be as simple as noticing or finding something that others have overlooked. Ultimately, the explorer thirsts for questions, not answers. It can become a personal journey, quest, and, ultimately, transformation. One's process of transformation does not depend on the actual physical journey but may begin with training and preparation. Same, too, with maintaining one's edge.

Soon after getting married, my wife and I became parents. Priorities changed and my adventures took a backseat to family responsibilities. No problem: if I couldn't get to the woods as often as before, I would bring the woods to me. Thus began an intense period of planting trees, placing tons of stone, and creating an outdoor training area (including a small waterfall, stream, and pond). By training outside, I endured and mentally normalized the cold, hot, rain, dark, etc., keeping me acclimated and physically prepared. Nowadays, despite kids older and fully independent, my daily predawn training sessions continue occur outside, regardless of weather. I don't have to go there to *be* there. Even better, others can enjoy my creation (even those with more relaxed ambitions).

The deliverance of adventure isn't in the departure, but in one's return home, better than before ~

Being there isn't just to know its success or capture its picture-perfect moment. It is having gotten there via the entire spectrum of obstacles, struggles, flops, discoveries, accomplishments, friendships, hidden wisdoms … until understanding it's not what you get, but what you *give* … that your success in exploring isn't in what you find, but in becoming *found*. When they ask you 'Where have you been?', tell them you have been overcoming failure, turning weakness into strength, moving forward despite illness, injury, exhaustion, or age … assisting others in reaching the finish despite hardships and mishaps, learning to shrug off a fall, getting back up … and revealing yourself to meaning. That is the voyage … and, even upon the waters of trial and tribulation, by building the ships of kinship, fellowship, leadership, and mentorship, we become unsinkable. May that place be where you are, go, and have *BEEN* !

For the world will otherwise

Impose and define you

Seek adventure

Push into challenge

Embrace awe

Become your own expression

Become your art

… your discipline

Cultivate within you

That beyond words

ABOUT THE AUTHOR

BRIAN S. WOODS (b.1965)...

Born in Charlotte, North Carolina, Woods was soon raised in the remote Appalachian Mountains of Virginia. A current healthcare executive, Woods is a lifelong student of combatives and a former Nuclear Security Police Officer for an entity serving the U.S. Naval Nuclear Propulsion Program, NASA, and other clients. Woods is a graduate of East Tennessee State University, where he earned Bachelor of Science degrees in both Political Science and Criminal Justice/Criminology. A black belt in several styles of Karate, Woods is a lifelong trekker and caver, and a 43-

year member of the National Speleological Society and founder of CAMEL Team Ops ('CAMEL' acronym for CAve Mountain ELements').

From an early age, Woods tested himself both physically and mentally, commonly engaging in extreme hardships alone, having access to thousands of acres of sparsely inhabited land. By the age of nine, Woods was exploring caves, searching for fossils, and running long distances through local woodlands. These traits prompted his parents to provide him with unique experiences and formal, specialized training. Early influential contacts included renowned caver, Roy D. Powers, Jr. and Colonel John H. Reeves, professor of biology at Virginia Military Institute. For several years, Woods was sponsored by the Big Stone Gap Virginia Dogwood Garden Club to attend Nature Camp, Inc., located in the George Washington National Forest near Vesuvius, Virginia. A two-week study of natural sciences, Woods was chosen Best Camper in 1982. Woods began weightlifting at age 13 and competed in wrestling and track for Powell Valley High School, where he was chosen as his wrestling team's MVP in 1983.

Though Woods' wrestling career ended after a severe wrist injury, his disciplined, multi-aspect approach to training continued. Initially, Woods combined high-intensity training with frequent challenges through rugged terrain and severe environments. By the early-1990's, Woods began training in martial arts, eventually earning black belts in Isshinryu Karate, Senido Karate and Cata Pon Jutsu, a style fusing martial arts with strength training, intense physical conditioning, tactical weapons training, and wilderness agility. Woods is still known for his intense outdoor training sessions, regardless of weather conditions.

A prolific lyricist, Woods authored *The Codex Bellum: Iron Wrapped In Cotton*, as well as *POMMEL: The Continuous Cut*.

THE CODEX BELLUM is a self-development guide on improving tangible & intangible strengths, developing greater tactical awareness, and with an overall theme that, for the warrior-archetype, through self-discipline, entwined with pursuing, improving, or defending larger causes, one becomes 'found' by meaning.

POMMEL is an often poetic-work of fantasy-fiction, much-inspired by Joseph Campbell's template of the hero's journey.

In 2011, Woods created a personal training business that, at the time, was considered an innovative fusion of tactical and fitness training. Called *TA Trainers* ('TA' acronym for Tactical Athletics), it was retooled and renamed CAMEL Team Ops in 2017. Members are described as 'highly trained ambassadors of the spirit of exploration' and have traveled internationally to engage the world's most wondrous terrain.

Woods and Penelope Smith were married in 1999. Currently, they reside near Johnson City, Tennessee

If you enjoyed **B E E N**, please check out my other books (via Amazon) …

The Codex Bellum: Iron Wrapped In Cotton

For those compelled by an inner, often insensible calling to seek challenge, embrace adversity, and become 'found' by meaning ... The Codex Bellum serves as a guide so that one may successfully navigate a vigorous lifestyle, understand combatives & tactical thinking, develop intangible strengths, and achieve a fitness of presence. Though the Codex Bellum is a book of physical, mental, and tactical intelligence, it is ultimately a journey of self-evolution. Beginning with one's mindset and body, The Codex Bellum turns to combating adversity until, finally, it advances into engaging dynamics and interaction with an encompassed and worldly vision.

POMMEL Trilogy: The Continuous Cut

"POMMEL is a futuristic narrative, written towards the simplicity of an old Viking tale ..." From a post-apocalyptic world comes a tale set in the mold of Joseph Campbell's timeless hero's journey. Orphaned and outcast from his homeland, Lineadia, Pommel for years aimlessly experiences the rugged hardships of life until his true character finally emerges. Along with a ragged band of characters, Pommel challenges the scourge of the land: his childhood rival, Saint Clair. In a series of twists and adventures, Pommel forges a path of self-discovery, while transforming himself from warrior to hero.

Might there be future books of

BEEN

?

You never know … perhaps … until then,

KEEP EXPLORING